Soil

Melissa Stewart

Heinemann
LIBRARY

www.heinemann.co.uk/library
Visit our website to find out more information about Heinemann Library books.

To order:
 Phone 44 (0) 1865 888066
 Send a fax to 44 (0) 1865 314091
Visit the Heinemann Bookshop at www.heinemann.co.uk/library to browse our catalogue and order online.

First published in Great Britain by Heinemann Library, Halley Court, Jordan Hill, Oxford OX2 8EJ
a division of Reed Educational and Professional Publishing Ltd. Heinemann is a registered trademark
of Reed Educational and Professional Publishing Ltd.

OXFORD MELBOURNE AUCKLAND JOHANNESBURG BLANTYRE
GABORONE IBADAN PORTSMOUTH (NH) USA CHICAGO

Produced for Heinemann Library by Editorial Directions
Designed by Ox and Company
Originated by Ambassador Litho Ltd
Printed in Hong Kong

ISBN 0 431 14376 5
06 05 04 03 02
10 9 8 7 6 5 4 3 2 1

British Library Cataloguing in Publication Data
Stewart, Melissa
Soil. – (Rocks and minerals)
1. Soils – Juvenile literature
I. Title
552.5

Acknowledgements
The Publishers would like to thank the following for permission to reproduce photographs:

Photographs ©: Cover background, A.J. Copley/Visuals Unlimited, Inc.; cover foreground, Lester V. Bergman/Corbis; p. 4,
James P. Rowan; p. 5, Scott Berner/Visuals Unlimited, Inc.; p. 7, Jack K. Clark/The Image Works; p. 8, Dick Keen/Visuals
Unlimited, Inc.; p. 9, James P. Rowan; p. 10, Ken Lucas/Visuals Unlimited, Inc.; pp. 11, 12, A.J. Copley/Visuals Unlimited,
Inc.; p. 13, Tom & Therisa Stack/Tom Stack & Associates; p. 16, A.J. Copley/Visuals Unlimited, Inc.; p. 18, Tom
Smart/Gamma Liaison/Hulton Archive; p. 20, James P. Rowan; p. 21, Mark Wilson/Newsmakers/Gamma Liaison/Hulton
Archive; p. 22, A.J. Copley/Visuals Unlimited, Inc.; p. 23, Reuters New Media, Inc./Corbis; p. 24, Tom Bean; p. 25, Joe
McDonald/Tom Stack & Associates; p. 26, John D. Cunningham/Visuals Unlimited, Inc.; p. 27, Rob & Ann
Simpson/Simpson's Nature Photography; p. 28, Patrick Aventurier/Gamma Liaison/Hulton Archive; p. 29, Ken Lucas/Visuals
Unlimited, Inc.

Our thanks to Martin Lawrence and Alan Timms of the Natural History Museum, London for their assistance in the
preparation of this edition.

Contents

Any words appearing in the text in bold, **like this**, are explained in the Glossary.

What is soil?

This girl is taking a look at the soil in her garden. It is a good place to grow flowers and vegetables.

If you go outside and dig up a small patch of grass, what do you think you will see underneath? You will see soil, of course. Maybe you've wondered whether dirt and soil are exactly the same. Actually, there is a difference.

The word 'soil' is used only to describe the material that covers the Earth's surface. The word 'dirt' can be used to describe soil or anything that is not clean. Animal waste is sometimes called dirt, and so is dust. Dust is a mixture of soil particles, strands of hair, dead insect parts, food crumbs and other things. Dust even contains flakes of skin that have worn off our bodies!

EATING SOIL!

For thousands of years, certain groups of people have eaten soil. They think it can bring good luck. Scientists admit that soil can provide **nutrients** that some people may not get from the foods they eat. But that's no reason to scoop up a handful of soil and pop it into your mouth. Eating soil could make you very sick – it could even kill you!

Look closely

Have you ever taken a really close look at soil
and wondered what it is made of? Soil is made of
broken-up rocks, water, air and bits of rotting
material. An average soil sample can contain
about 45 per cent broken-up rocks, 25 per cent
water, 25 per cent air, and 5 per cent rotting
material, although these percentages vary.

Where does the rotting material come from?
When leaves and twigs fall to the ground, they
slowly rot, or decay, and become part of the soil.
Animal waste gradually breaks down and
becomes part of the soil, too. All living things
become part of the soil when they die.

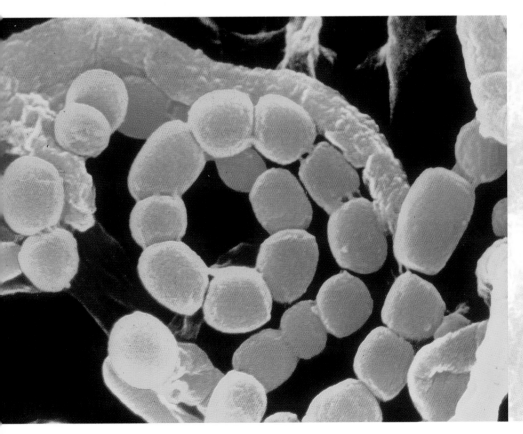

DID YOU KNOW?

Soil provides a good
meal and a safe
home for many living
things. Some of these
creatures are so
small that you need
a microscope to see
them, such as the
soil **bacteria** shown
here. Believe it or
not, there can be
more of these tiny
creatures in one
spoonful of soil
than the number
of people living on the
Earth – billions!

How does soil form?

All soil begins as solid rock. Most rock forms slowly over millions of years. Even though it may seem very tough, as soon as it forms, natural forces begin to break rock apart. Over time, giant boulders gradually become small stones, then gravel, then pebbles, and then sand or even smaller particles. When these tiny bits of rock mix with water, air and other materials, new soil is created.

Waves and water currents slowly erode a lake's rocky shore. Over time, giant boulders break down and form the lake's sandy bottom.

Erosion

Crashing ocean waves, spreading glaciers, whipping winds and other natural forces slowly **erode** rock on the Earth's surface. Rocks may also break up as they bump into one another in fast-flowing streams. Rock deep underground can be eroded by seeping rainwater.

DID YOU KNOW?

Soil forms slowly, but it can be destroyed quickly. It can take more than 500 years to form 2.5 centimetres of soil, but a ferocious storm can wash away that soil in just a few minutes. Farmers know erosion can do a lot of damage to their fields, so they take various measures to protect this precious resource.

Even the Earth's tallest mountains are affected by the power of erosion.

Weathering

A process called **weathering** can also break down rock. Sometimes, plant roots grow into a rock's cracks, pushing and eventually splitting it. Repeated freezing and thawing can cause a rock to shrink and expand. Over time, this may weaken a rock and cause it to crumble into pieces. Boulders, pebbles and sand were once part of much larger rocks!

Wind and sand have eroded these large rocks in the US state of Wyoming. Weathering has caused visible cracks.

Soil covers the Earth

A handful of soil reveals many things: bits of rock, plant roots, rotting materials and tiny creatures. The colour and texture tell you what type of soil it is.

Soil covers most of the Earth's surface. It lies under lush forests and dry deserts, tall buildings and winding roads, and there are even **sediments** at the bottom of the oceans. The only places without soil are the tops of tall mountains and places so cold that they are made of solid ice. In some areas, the soil is a few centimetres thick. In others, it can be a metre deep. The amount of soil in an area depends on the weather and the mixture of materials near by.

DID YOU KNOW?

The deep ocean is a cold, dark place. Few creatures can survive in such a harsh environment. The sediments along the ocean floor build up slowly over time. It is littered with millions of tiny skeletons of animals that once lived closer to the water's surface. These skeletons take much longer to break down than dead material on land.

Volcanoes

Some of the richest soils in the world are found near volcanoes. When a volcano erupts, it often releases huge quantities of ash and dust particles. These materials contain a variety of **nutrients** that help plants live and grow.

Plants need soil

We could not live without soil. The plants that grow in soil give us the food we eat and the oxygen we breathe. Rice, one of the most important crops in the world, grows in fields of wet soil called paddies. Lettuce, tomatoes, oranges, maize, grapes, carrots and peas all grow in soil.

Plants also provide us with shade on hot summer days and give us fuel to heat our homes during long, cold winters. Some important medicines come from plants that grow in tropical rainforest soils.

Other materials come from plants, too. The cotton in your T-shirts grows on large farms in warm parts of the world, like Egypt or Turkey. The paper in this book was probably made from trees that grow in northern forests.

New plants are beginning to grow in this field in California in the USA. Much of California's richest soil is composed of materials that wash down from nearby mountains.

Layers of soil

ON THE LOOKOUT

You may be able to see layers of soil without digging down into the ground. The next time you take a country walk, look for **eroded** stream banks. Can you spot the different layers?

If you dig down into the ground, you will notice that the soil begins to change as you go deeper. Near the surface, the soil is dark brown and loosely packed, with very few large rocks. Deeper down, the soil has a lighter colour, is more tightly packed and is full of rocks. The soil is different because it forms in layers. The soil in the upper layers contains more materials than the soil in the lower layers.

Topsoil

The first few centimetres of soil are called **topsoil**. Topsoil is often dark brown and can have plenty of rotting material and tiny creatures mixed in, but it can be other colours, too.

Soil is constantly being created. The way the different layers of soil develop depends on the parent material, creatures in the soil, surface features, climate and time.

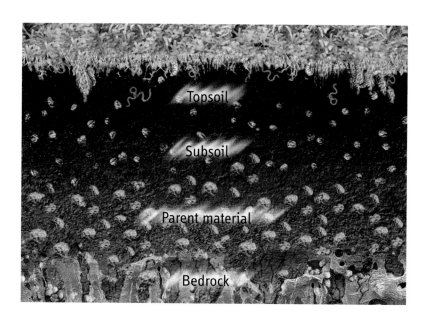

10

DID YOU KNOW?

Soil colours range from yellow and red to dark brown and black. The colour depends on the amount and types of rocks, rotting material, and living creatures in the soil.

Subsoil

The roots of most plants are found in this layer. All the materials and living things in topsoil help to keep it loosely packed with plenty of air pockets. When you rub certain topsoils between your fingers, they can feel soft and slightly spongy. Below the topsoil is a layer called the **subsoil**. Subsoil is usually lighter in colour. It has more rock and less rotting material than topsoil. It also has fewer spaces for air and water. When you rub certain subsoils between your fingers, they can feel a bit gritty.

Parent material

The **parent material** lies below the subsoil. It has no rotting material at all and is more tightly packed than the layers above it. The parent is usually made up of a weathered rocky mass. The rocks and gravel have chipped off the solid **bedrock** below the parent material.

Soil texture

The bits of rock that make up soil can be grouped into three sizes – large, medium, and small. The largest bits are called sand. You can see plenty of sand on the beach at the seaside. The medium-size bits are called silt. The smallest bits are called clay. You need an electron microscope to see individual grains of clay.

This sunny beach is covered with countless pieces of tiny soil particles called sand. Most plants do not grow well in sandy soil, but certain grassy species can survive.

Desert soil

Most plants do not grow well in sandy soil. Rainwater drains through sand so quickly that plants dry up. Desert soil is very sandy, but cactuses can still grow in deserts because they have special ways of holding onto water. Their spiny leaves lose less water to **evaporation** than do the broad leaves of plants in fields and forests. Also, cactus stems can store large quantities of water, and their roots fan out in every direction. A saguaro cactus's roots may be more than 23 metres long.

DID YOU KNOW?

In the late 1880s, the Denver and Rio Grande Western Railroad in the American West gave the name Silt to a town in Colorado. The town was named after the soil in the area, which made it difficult to lay tracks.

The stems of the rare organ pipe cactus can hold many gallons of water. It grows only in the Sonoran Desert areas of Mexico and the US state of Arizona.

Water in soil

Soils that contain more silt and clay are better for growing plants because these soils hold more rainwater. But soil that has no sand in it may drain so slowly that plant roots start to rot.

Plants grow best in soils with plenty of rotting material and equal parts of sand, silt, and clay. This kind of soil is called **loam**.

	WHAT KIND OF SOIL DO YOU HAVE?	
SOIL TYPE	WHEN DRY SOIL IS SQUEEZED	WHEN WET SOIL IS SQUEEZED
Sand	Feels gritty, falls apart	Holds together, but crumbles easily
Silt	Feels smooth and silky, holds together	Holds together and does not crumble easily, but cannot be rolled into a long, snake-shaped strand
Clay	Feels slippery or sticky, breaks into hard clumps	Holds together and can be rolled into a long, snake-shaped strand

A look at humus

The dense plant life in this forest provides rotting material for humus. In turn, the humus supplies the plants with important nutrients.

Farmers and scientists use the word **humus** to describe the bits of rotting material in the upper layers of soil. Humus is usually dark brown or black and is full of the **nutrients** that plants need to live and grow. Like glue, humus helps hold together the bits of rock in soil. Like a sponge, humus soaks up water and holds onto it.

DID YOU KNOW?

Farmers in North America's Great Plains grow rye, oats and barley as well as wheat and maize. All these plants are kinds of grasses that grow well in the soil of that region.

The amount of humus in soil has a lot to do with the kinds of plants that grow in an area. The soil in forests is usually rich in humus. Grasslands also have rich soil. Natural grasslands support many kinds of grasses, some trees and a rich variety of wildflowers.

Great grasslands

North American prairie grasslands are home to pronghorns, buffalo, prairie dogs and many birds and insects. Lions, zebras, giraffes and elephants live on the savannah grasslands in Africa.

The Great Plains grasslands of North America have some of the best soil in the world. American and Canadian farmers harvest tonnes of maize and wheat in these areas every year. The maize is used to feed cattle and people. The wheat is used in many popular foods, including breakfast cereals, pasta, bread, cakes and biscuits.

Peat

Some swamps and most bogs have a kind of soil called peat. Peat contains more humus and less rocky material than other soils. It can hold a lot of water and is good for growing plants such as cranberries, peat moss and Venus's-flytraps.

For many years, people thought swamps, marshes and other wetlands were useless. Now we know that the soils and plants in wetlands can remove pollutants and other harmful chemicals from the water.

HOW PEOPLE USE PEAT

In some parts of the world, people burn peat to keep warm. Some people cut the peat themselves, while others buy it. When the humus-rich soil is added to other kinds of soils, plants thrive. Peat bogs are getting quite rare, so peat use needs to be carefully managed and some peat areas need to be protected by law.

Tiny soil creatures

Most soil contains billions of creatures so small that you need a microscope to see them. These tiny living things include **bacteria** and **fungi**. Bacteria and fungi are not plants, but they are not animals either.

Bacteria are one-celled creatures that live for a few hours or a few days. They reproduce by splitting in half. Some bacteria cause deadly diseases, but most are harmless to humans. They can be found just about everywhere.

IMAGINE THAT!

No one knew that bacteria existed until the late 1600s when a Dutch cloth merchant named Anton van Leeuwenhoek (left) saw them in a simple microscope he had built. It took even longer for scientists to realize that some bacteria make people ill. They can cause tooth decay, tonsillitis, scarlet fever, impetigo and other illnesses. Today, doctors use drugs called antibiotics to kill the bacteria that make us ill.

Fungi are living things belonging to a group that includes moulds, yeasts and other creatures. Most fungi live underground, so you never see them. But you may have seen mushrooms, puffballs, or stinkhorns in woodlands. Their structures help the fungi reproduce, just as flowers help plants reproduce.

Most fungi live underground. When conditions are right, some produce mushrooms that release spores, so more fungi can grow in new places.

Bacteria and fungi at work

Bacteria and fungi have a very important job to do. They make **humus** by consuming tonnes of autumn leaves, the flesh of dead animals, and even each other. As these tiny creatures break down materials, they return vital **nutrients** to the soil.

Without bacteria and fungi, nothing on the Earth would decay. Nutrients would never get back into the soil, and plants would not grow in soil without nutrients. If there were no plants on the Earth, animals – including humans – would have nothing to eat. Bacteria and fungi may be small, but they are an important part of every **ecosystem** in the world.

DID YOU KNOW?

In cold parts of the world, many of the tiny creatures that live in the soil become inactive during the winter.

Plants in the soil

Grassland soils are rich in nutrients. They can support an abundance of plant life, such as the Blazing Star shown in this US prairie.

Almost all plants need soil to grow. Most plants grow best in warm, moist soil that has plenty of **humus**, a variety of tiny living creatures and a mixture of sand, silt and clay. That is why more plants live in the world's forests, grasslands and wetlands than in dry deserts or on the chilly **tundra** of the far north. The humus and rocky materials in soil give plants all the **nutrients** they need to live, grow and make flowers. Without energy from the Sun and nutrients from the soil, plants could not produce the leaves, nuts and fruits that cows, zebras, elephants and other animals eat.

THAT'S INCREDIBLE!

Some plants do not grow in soil. They get all the nutrients they need from water and air. Duckweed and water hyacinths live in stagnant ponds and lakes. Their roots dangle a few inches below the water's surface, but they do not touch the bottom. Spanish moss and some orchids are air plants. They hang from the branches of tall trees.

The meat eaters, such as wolves, lions, jaguars, eagles and owls, hunt the plant eaters for food. As a result, meat-eating **predators** depend on plants, too. Plants are an important part of every **ecosystem** on the Earth. Without soil to grow plants, many living things would not survive.

Stopping erosion

Plants take nutrients from the soil, but they also help the soil. The roots of plants in fields and forests grow down into the soil and help hold it together. As a result, less soil is **eroded** by the wind and rain.

Plants that grow in wetlands prevent flooding and often remove dangerous poisons from the soil. As plant roots grow downward, they sometimes force themselves into tiny cracks and crevices in rocks. Over time, the roots break up the rocks and help make new soil.

DID YOU KNOW?

The rafflesia plant of Malaysia (right) produces the largest flowers in the world. Like other plants, it could not produce such large blossoms if it did not get plenty of nutrients from the soil it grows in.

Animals in the soil

Animals need soil to survive. The grass that horses, zebras, cattle and sheep feed on grows in soil, as do the fruits and seeds that many birds eat. Without soil, there would be no brightly coloured flowers with sugary nectar to feed bees, hummingbirds and butterflies.

Living in soil

Large groups of prairie dogs live together in communities called 'towns'. The animals in each town dig a huge network of underground tunnels in the soil.

The soil also provides a safe home for many kinds of animals. In some parts of the world, 0.4 hectare of soil can support five to ten tonnes of living creatures. Many slugs, beetles, flatworms, and millipedes spend their entire lives in soil. They find plenty of food there. Badgers, chipmunks, rabbits, skunks, and prairie dogs sleep and hide from enemies in underground burrows. Many other creatures, such as hedgehogs, dormice and gophers, spend the coldest months of winter **hibernating** in the soil.

Animals are also important to the soil. Grazing animals leave **manure** behind.

When **bacteria** and **fungi** break down the manure, they add a variety of **nutrients** to the soil. During the summer, mice, moles and shrews plow through the soil in search of food. Beetles, centipedes and earthworms also make trails through the soil. Air and water can fill the spaces these animals leave behind. Plant roots need this air and water.

DID YOU KNOW?

Have you ever seen a very bumpy lawn? All those lumps and bumps were probably made by energetic moles as they tunnelled through the soil in search of insects and tasty plant roots. Some types of moles spend so much of their lives underground that they are blind or have no eyes.

INCREDIBLE EARTHWORMS

As earthworms wriggle through the soil, they suck up all the soil in their path. In fact, a single earthworm 'eats' several pounds of soil each year. The waste materials that earthworms leave behind are called 'casts'. Casts are full of nutrients. Scientists can tell how healthy the soil is by looking at the earthworms living in it. If the soil has too much water or too few nutrients, the earthworms look pale.

Nutrients in the soil

This worker is spraying a field of maize with liquid fertilizer. While fertilizers provide crops with needed nutrients, they can also pollute groundwater.

Plants get the **nutrients** they need from the soil. Some nutrients come from **humus**. Others come from the **minerals** in rocky particles of sand, silt and clay. Sometimes plants use up the nutrients in soil faster than new ones are created, so farmers often add fertilizers containing nitrogen and phosphorus to their fields.

Rabbits are plant eaters. They feed on a wide range of grasses.

Cycle of nutrients

When a plant-eating animal, such as a rabbit, eats grass, the nutrients in the plant enter the rabbit's body. The rabbit uses the nutrients to grow and keep its heart, brain and muscles working. When a meat eater, such as a fox, eats the rabbit, some of the nutrients become part of the fox's body.

The fox uses these important chemicals to make its body work. When it dies, **bacteria**, **fungi** and other small organisms go to work on its carcass. In just a few weeks, they break down the **predator's** body, and the nutrients are returned to the soil. In this way, nutrients cycle through an **ecosystem**.

NUTRIENTS AND THE LIFE CYCLE

NUTRIENT	WHAT IT DOES FOR PLANTS	WHAT IT DOES FOR ANIMALS
Calcium	Helps plants take in other nutrients, helps roots and leaves grow	Helps animals make bones and teeth and keeps them strong
Magnesium	Helps plants use sunlight to make food	Helps animals keep their hearts and blood vessels healthy
Nitrogen	Helps plants grow and stay green	Not used directly by animals
Phosphorus	Helps plants make flowers, fruits and seeds	Helps animals keep their brains and nerves working, helps break down vitamins
Potassium	Helps plants fight diseases	Helps animals keep their muscles strong and healthy, helps keep blood flowing

How do people use soil?

This farm in the US state of Texas was abandoned because all the **topsoil** eroded during the Dust Bowl of the 1930s. The plants farmers were trying to grow could not survive a period of severe droughts.

Amongst other crops, farmers grow wheat, corn and vegetables in the soil. The plants farmers feed to cattle, pigs and other animals also grow in soil. Farmers know it is important to keep the soil rich.

FARMING IN DELTAS

A delta is a piece of land where a river deposits mud, sand and gravel as it flows into a larger body of water. The word 'delta' comes from the Greek letter delta (Δ), because of the triangle shape of many deltas. The soil in a delta is made of clay, sand and silt. This soil is full of nutrients. All the nutrients make the delta soil an excellent place for farming. For thousands of years, fertile delta lands around the world have been used by farmers to grow their crops.

The River Nile in Egypt, the Brahmaputra and Ganges Rivers in India, and the Mississippi River in Louisiana have some of the world's largest deltas.

Looking after soil

Many farmers add fertilizer and try to prevent the land from **eroding**. Some farmers also rotate their crops. Because different plants require different **nutrients**, rotating crops each year means the soil can continue to grow healthy plants season after season.

Soil in use

People also use soil in other ways. Artists use clay to make pottery. Before they start shaping the clay, they dry it, crush it, and strain it. This gets rid of unwanted materials in the clay. Sand can be used to make glass and explosives and to filter water. It is also an important ingredient in many building materials, including cement, concrete, mortar and plaster.

Some people use adobe to build houses. Adobe, a mixture of soil, straw and water, is poured into moulds and dried to make bricks. Most adobe houses are coated with plaster to keep the adobe dry.

An ancient tribe of Native Americans in New Mexico, USA built this adobe pueblo, or dwelling, about 800 years ago. Adobe falls apart if it gets wet, so it is only used in areas with low rainfall.

Studying soil

When you see soil from a distance, it may seem like nothing more than a dark brown, lumpy material. But soil is more interesting than you might think. Have you ever run your fingers through soil to see how it feels? Have you ever smelled soil? If not, it's time to give it a try.

A sieve can help you separate the materials in soil. You can make your own sieve by putting fine wire mesh in a frame or box.

Try it yourself

Take a spade and dig up some soil and spread it on a newspaper. Make sure you get permission first. You may want to use a **sieve** to separate the materials that make up the soil. Look at the soil closely with a hand lens. You will see some pebbles and tiny bits of rock. You may also see pieces of rotting plants. Do you see any insects or earthworms? What else is in your soil sample? Be sure to write down everything you observe.

DID YOU KNOW?

Ped is the Latin word for 'foot', so you could think of pedologists as scientists who study the material found beneath our feet.

Now go to another spot and dig up some soil there. Compare the two samples.

When you have studied both soil samples, return the soil to the ground, clean your tools and put them away. Always wash your hands thoroughly when you have been handling soil.

Soil scientists

Some scientists spend many hours studying and classifying soil. They record where the soil was found and the different materials in it. These scientists are called **pedologists**.

Pedologists can help farmers decide what crops they should grow in certain types of soil. They can also recommend things that can be added to the soil to make it just right for growing a particular kind of plant.

PUTTING SCIENCE TO WORK

For many years, soil engineers in Pisa, Italy, have been studying the layers of topsoil and subsoil around the Leaning Tower of Pisa. They have now taken steps to stabilize the tower so that it does not tip any further.

Sources of soil

This woman is inspecting young fir trees. Soon they will be planted in a forest area as part of a reforestation plan.

Soil is a **natural resource**. Wood, iron and oil are also natural resources. We use all these materials to make important products, like paper, cars, plastics and petrol.

Careful use

Iron and oil are nonrenewable natural resources. Once we use up nonrenewable resources, we cannot replace them. But trees are a renewable natural resource, and so is soil. It takes many years for most varieties of trees to grow, but if we replant them carefully, we will never run out of trees. People can also create more soil – but it takes quite a bit of time and effort. People need to be careful not to use up trees and soil faster than they can be replaced.

Making soil

You may know someone who makes his or her own soil. Many people who like to grow flowers or vegetables make **compost** for their gardens. Instead of throwing away plant materials, they use them to create compost. Compost is the dark, crumbly mixture created from the rotting plant material. Unlike **humus**, it does not contain the remains of animals.

Compost can be made from fallen leaves, grass clippings and vegetable and fruit scraps from the kitchen. While it is rotting, the material needs to be kept moist, but not too wet. As compost forms, the **nutrients** from the plants break down. When compost is mixed with soil, new plants can absorb those nutrients, helping them to grow.

Starting a garden compost pile is a great idea. With a little patience, you can turn kitchen scraps and colourful autumn leaves into a nutrient-rich material that will help plants grow.

Glossary

bacteria tiny living things that may feed on rotting material. Some bacteria can make people sick.

bedrock layer of solid rock just below the soil

compost mixture of rotting plant material that adds nutrients to soil

ecosystem community of living things and their environment

erode to slowly wear away over time by the action of wind, water or glaciers

evaporation process that changes a liquid into a gas

friction force that resists motion between two objects or surfaces

fungus living thing that is neither a plant nor an animal. The plural of fungus is fungi.

hibernating resting or sleeping for the winter

humus rotting material in soil

loam fertile soil containing sand, silt and some clay

manure the droppings of animals that can enrich the soil

mineral natural solid material with a specific chemical makeup and structure

natural resource natural material that humans use to make important products

nutrient natural chemical that plants and animals need for their bodies to work properly

parent material bottom layer of soil. It contains large pieces of gravel and rock, but no humus.

pedologist scientist who studies and classifies soil

predator animal that hunts and kills other animals for food

sieve strainer, or filter, used to separate tiny pieces from large ones

subsoil middle layer of soil. It contains larger pieces of rock and less humus than topsoil.

topsoil top layer of soil. It contains small bits or rock and large quantities of rotting material.

tundra ecosystem in the far north where summer is very short and only a few kinds of plants and animals can survive

weathering breaking down of rock by plant roots or by repeated freezing and thawing

Further information

BOOKS

New Star Science: Rocks and Soil, Ginn, 2001

Rocks, Minerals and Soil, BJ Knapp, Atlantic Europe, 2001

Rocks, Soil and Weather, Nuffield Primary Science, Collins Educational, 1995

ORGANIZATIONS

Soil Survey and Land Research Centre
www.silsoe.cranfield.ac.uk/sslrc
Cranfield University
Bedford MK45 4DT
UK

CSIRO Land and Water
www.clw.csiro.au
University Road
Townsville
Queensland
Australia

International Erosion Control Association
www.ieca.org
P.O. Box 774904
1355 S. Lincoln Avenue
Steamboat Springs, Colorado 80477
USA

Soil and Water Conservation Society
www.swcs.org
7515 N.E. Ankeny Road
Ankeny, Iowa 50021
USA

Index

Titles in the *Rocks and Minerals* series include:

Hardback   0 431 14370 6

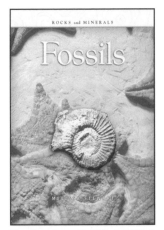

Hardback   0 431 14371 4

Hardback   0 431 14372 2

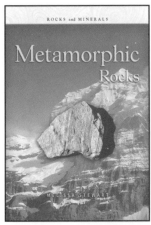

Hardback   0 431 14373 0

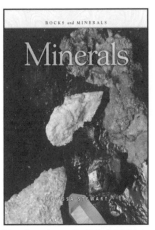

Hardback   0 431 14374 9

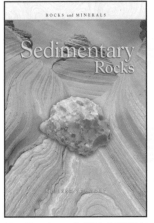

Hardback   0 431 14375 7

Hardback   0 431 14376 5

Find out about the other titles in this series on our website www.heinemann.co.uk/library